M L.
Rea

26
AM   58
INSPIRING DEVOTIONAL
PROGRAMS FOR WOMEN'S GROUPS

DO NOT REMOVE
CARDS FROM POCKET

Inspiring Devotional Programs For Women's Groups

by

LEILA T. AMMERMAN

BAKER BOOK HOUSE
Grand Rapids, Michigan

Copyright 1960 by Baker Book House Company

Library of Congress Catalog Card Number: 60-15264

ISBN: 0-8010-0015-7

First printing, February 1971
Second printing, November 1972
Third printing, November 1975
Fourth printing, September 1977
Fifth printing, September 1979
Sixth printing, October 1981
Seventh printing, January 1984

PHOTOLITHOPRINTED BY CUSHING - MALLOY, INC.
ANN ARBOR, MICHIGAN, UNITED STATES OF AMERICA

CONTENTS

CONTENTS	THEME	PAGE
FOREWORD	7068358	5
THREE "P's" FOR ADULT CLASSES		7
SIMPLE INSTALLATION SERVICE		10
JANUARY MEETING	BEAUTY	13
FEBRUARY MEETING	SELF-CONTROL	16
MARCH MEETING	GENTLENESS	20
APRIL MEETING	JOY	24
MAY MEETING	PRAISE	27
JUNE MEETING	FAITH	30
JULY MEETING	LOYALTY	33
AUGUST MEETING	ENDURANCE	36
SEPTEMBER MEETING	WISDOM	39
OCTOBER MEETING	COURAGE	42
NOVEMBER MEETING	THANKFULNESS	45
DECEMBER MEETING	HOPE	48

SUPPLEMENTAL PROGRAMS

No. 1	TRUST	51
No. 2	GROWTH	53
No. 3	SONG	57
No. 4	NEW LIFE	58
No. 5	IN THE BEGINNING	60

FOREWORD

It is our sincere hope that this book will fill a need for resource materials with which to build a worthwhile program for adult monthly class meetings.

The materials are chosen with the hope that they may be adapted for use by adults of many ages; in many different situations; and many different sized groups.

Do you prefer to plan your own simple refreshments and decorations? Then ignore that section — it is for some seeking help in that field. You do not use games at your class meetings? Then ignore them — they are included for those classes that do use them.

The materials are set up so that you may use, or leave out, any parts as you wish. They are suggestions that perhaps may start your own thinking.

All Scripture references are from the Revised Standard Version of the Bible. Hymn numbers are from "Christian Worship — A Hymnal".

This little book may be invaluable as help for officers and teachers in planning programs —— and in enlisting hostesses.

This is our aim.

Leila Tremaine Ammerman

THREE "P's" FOR ADULT CLASSES

The class which prays together and works together will grow together.

So you teach (or are a member of) an adult class in the Sunday School, and you want to know the ways by which you can make that group of adults effective in kingdom building? You would like to bring the class to new vitality, and make it a part of the Sunday Church School that will be progressive and vital in the Church's program.

Just as there are "three R's" in secular education, there are "three P's" in the formation of a really vital adult class. We list them in the order of their use and effectiveness. Prayer, projects, and progress, are the three steps in the growth of a vital class.

PRAYER

First, an effective adult class must have a definite program of prayer. It is very important that Christians continue throughout their lives to grow in the ability to pray. The teacher of an adult class has an obligation to the members, and to God — to lead all within it to the place where they are willing to lead the class in public prayer.

It is a wonderful thing for a class to set aside a few moments each Sunday to pray together for some specific person or project that they may visualize. Ask each member of the class alternately to bring to the attention of the class some person or project on the various Sundays of the year. This moment of prayer may be a moment of silence, when all the members pray for the Sunday's project; or the person who brings the suggestion for prayer may lead the group in prayer on the subject.

It will be quite surprising to find how much more important things become when a group prays together to achieve them. No one need ever be at a loss for some worthy cause for which to pray. Nearly every Protestant church has missionaries at home and abroad who may be prayed for individuallyy. Appeals for cancer, polio, t. b., crippled children or Red Cross are always before us, as are the poor and diseased in the far corners of the globe. It may be a personal friend in sorrow or trouble, for whom we would ask the prayers of the class. Do not be surprised if the interest in missions and charities grows in proportion to the amount of prayer!

PROJECTS

This idea of a few moments of "special" prayer each Sunday morning leads right into the second "P" of a vital adult class — service projects. If you want a class that is alive and interested in the affairs of the church — give them something at which to which to work for others, each Sunday of the year.

Projects may be large or small, but it is always a good idea to have a large, long-range project under way, while at the same time you may be accomplishing little, near at home projects.

1. An adult class can be a wonderful "pastoral assistant" if they will undertake steady year-around evangelistic calling on behalf of the church. Any pastor will welcome the offer for members of the class to make a certain number of calls each month on delinquent church members or prospects for memberships.

2. Calling on the sick and shut-ins is a wonderful ministry to undertake at any time. Even telephoning to those who are ill, or having a member responsible for sending get-well cards, will be greatly appreciated by the recipients.

3. Baskets of food for the poor of your own community at holiday time (and perhaps even more important — a bag of groceries now and then throughout the year) can be a blessing which any adult class can achieve.

4. Sometimes there is actual work with the hands that is needed in the church school building. Perhaps the tiny chairs or playpens in the nursery have become marred and marked. A bit of bright paint can do wonders. This calls for a work party some afternoon or evening when the members may meet and work together.

The list of projects that may be undertaken is endless, and I will guarantee that your "Project Committee' will always have more work ahead, and ideas stored away than you ever quite finish. This is as it should be. Anyone with eyes to see can find need which may be met by a working adult class.

PROGRESS

An adult class that is working together and praying together progresses and grows. Any class that recognizes prayer as the first and most essential part of its program will be receptive to the lessons from the Bible each Sunday. Every class that has important service projects under way at all times will grow and *grow* and *GROW!* The very idea of service for others will come through the weekly practice of "special" prayer, and through prayer and projects will come a progress you had never dreamed possible!

INSTALLATION SERVICE FOR CLASS OFFICERS

This is a simple installation service, in which the outgoing and ingoing officers take part together. If there is more than one officer in any of the offices, let them speak together, and substitute the plural pronoun (as "we" for "I") and the service will be adequate.

A small table should be centered against a wall, with an open Bible placed upon it. One large white candle and five smaller white candles (or as many as needed for your officers) should be ready in holders. The outgoing President holds the large lighted candle and takes his place beside the table. Give each of the new officers one of the small candles, unlighted. The outgoing President speaks:

OUTGOING PRESIDENT

This large candle represents our Lord, Jesus Christ. Through the past year we, the outgoing officers of the .... Class have striven to keep the light of His teaching bright within our hearts. We have tried to live rightly, and to help the class grow in knowledge, and understanding, and service.

We urge you, the new officers, to keep this light ever in your hearts, that you may truly lead the class in the path of righteousness, for His Name's sake.

(The outgoing President places the candlestick with the tall lighted candle on the table behind the open Bible, and takes a place at the extreme right of the table.)

INCOMING PRESIDENT:

(Taking a place at immediate left of the table) As the new President of the .... Class. I accept your challenge, and will strive with all my heart to perform the duties required of me. (He lights his small candle from the tall candle on the table. Then holds it high.) Jesus said: "I am the light of the world; he who follows me will not walk

in darkness, but will have the light of life." (John 8:12)
Only as our lives touch the life of Jesus do we find light that
brightens the dark places of the world. I would keep my
light shining that it may be a beacon to all men, to draw
them to the Father. I would be true to the office I am to
serve this coming year, with God's help.

INCOMING VICE PRESIDENT: (Taking place at right of
table)

As your new Vice President, I would pledge myself to stand
beside your President, helping in all ways that I am able,
to further the purposes of the .... Class, and to
strengthen our Christian living, that together we may grow
in grace. (He lights his small candle from the tall candle on
the table and holds it high.) Jesus said: "I have come as a
light into the world, that whoever believes in Me may not
remain in darkness." (John 12:46) We would have that
light in our lives, that we may help to lead the class in the
pathways of truth. I would be true to the office I am to
serve this coming year, with God's help.

INCOMING SECRETARY: (Taking place beside Incoming
President)

As Secretary of the .... Class, I would strive ever to
be a worthy leader, and to serve wherever needed. (He
lights his small candle from the tall candle on the table and
holds it high) Jesus said: "You are the light of world. A
city set on a hill cannot be hid." (Matt. 5:14)
We who are your leaders for the coming year will strive to
keep the light glowing, that we may follow our Lord, and
so do God's will here below. I, as your secretary, would be
true to the office I am to serve this coming year, with God's
help.

TREASURER: (Quietly taking place beside Vice President)
As your new treasurer, I would try to handle worthily the

11

things of this world, which will be my service. I will strive to be honest, generous, and trustworthy, and to serve in any way that I may, in this year to come. Jesus said: "Let your light so shine before men that they may see your good works and give glory to your Father who is in heaven." (Matthew 5:16) We, the officers for this coming year in the........ Class would try to be worthy instruments for the good works of the class, that all glory may be given to our Father in heaven. I would strive, as your Treasurer, to be true to the office I am to serve this coming year, with God's help.

INCOMING PIANIST: (Quietly taking place beside Secretary

As Pianist for the........Class, I will strive always to use my talents in any way that they may be a blessing to all. In the Scriptures we read: "As every man hath received the gift, even so minister the same one to another, as good stewards of the manifold grace of God." (I Peter 4:10) I will strive to be true to the office to which you have called me, with God's help.

OUTGOING PRESIDENT:

Will the members of the........Class please rise? Do you, as members of the .... Class, promise to support these, your officers for the coming year, that you may strive, together, to grow in grace and knowledge of our Lord? (Answer: "We do.")
Let us bow our heads in prayer.
Our Father, we stand humbly before Thee, asking that Thou wilt bless these, Thy servants, whom we have chosen to be our leaders for the coming year. Let their lives be a reflection of the Light from Thy Son, beckoning men to follow Him, and live lives of Christian service and righteousness. In Jesus' Name we pray. Amen.

12

THOUGHT FOR THE MONTH:

> "He has made everything beautiful in its time; also he
> has put eternity into man's mind, yet so that he cannot
> find out what God has done from the beginning to the
> end."   Ecclesiastes 3:11

HYMN: "God, Who Touchest Earth With Beauty   #315
SCRIPTURE READING: Job 38:19-33
MEDITATIVE THOUGHT: Beauty

Where shall we turn for the manifestation of God's love and
power except to the grandeur and beauty of the universe He
made? The beauty of winter is a lovely thing, reminding us of
God, and of His constant love and care for us.

Who has seen evergreen boughs heavily coated with sparkling
white snow, so that they bend in graceful lines toward the ground,
and not been conscious of the touch of God's hand? Who has
seen snow covered mountains like lazy giants in the winter sun
and not been reminded of the power of a God who could make
such a lovely world?

He grants to each season its beauty. The cold, clean beauty
of snow and frost and evergreens for the winter: the new, joyous
green of budding trees and young things in the spring: the
warmth of sun and stream and brilliant flowers in summer: and
the vivid foliage and falling leaves in autumn.

The seasons tell a story of LIFE, the youth of spring, the
maturity of summer, the old age of autumn, and the clean white
stillness of winter at the close — and all, in their beauty, speak
to us of God.

> The beauty of God lies all around,
> In the glory of drifted snow;
> The glory of God is manifest
> In the tides that ebb and flow.
> The beauty of God is a glowing thing,
> Of earth, and snow, and sky —
> A beauty that fills the lives of all,
> From cradle till day that we die.

PRAYER:

Our Father, we thank Thee for eyes to see the beauty Thou has put here in Thy world, and we thank Thee for hearts receptive to that beauty, that we may read the messages Thou hast written in the seasons, and out upon Thy far-flung mountainsides. We know that Thou hast made all things beautiful in their time, and we pray that we may keep our vision wide, to see and understand, and our hearts thankful for Thy many blessings and mercy toward us. In Jesus' Name we pray these things. Amen.

HYMN: "For The Beauty Of The Earth" #167

BENEDICTION

May the Lord bless us all with His beauty and His peace in our hearts and may we truly follow the Christian way of life, through the grace of our Lord, Jesus Christ. Amen

SUGGESTIONS FOR THE HOSTESS

DECORATIONS:

Use blue candles on the table, with a yellow ribbon bow tied to each one. Either use blue glass bells from Christmas ornaments, tied with yellow ribbons, or make blue bells out of construction paper, and hang grouped above the table.

REFRESHMENTS:

Jello-Ice Cream. Plain slices of sponge cake or gold cake. Mixed candies and nuts.

Make Jello — any fruit flavor, with 1 and one half cups of boiling water. Let cool, but do not set. Add 1 #2 Can Fruit Salad, drained, and 1 pint vanilla ice cream. Blend together and set in refrigerator to "jell". Recipe may be doubled or tripled as required.

GAMES: Bible Quiz

1. Which of the twelve disciples acted as treasurer?
(Answer: Judas)
2. What was Mose's rod turned into? (Answer: Serpent)
3. What boy had a coat of many colors? (Answer: Joseph)
4. What was the name of Abraham's wife? (Answer: Sarah)

14

5. Who was the "Weeping Prophet?"   (Answer: Jeremiah)
6. What prophet saw a wheel in a vision? (Answer: Ezekiel)
7. What king played a harp and wrote songs?

(Answer: David)

8. What famous queen visited Solomon?

(Answer: Queen of Sheba)

9. What prophet saw the Lord in the year Uzziah died?

(Answer: Isaiah)

10. What prophet was swallowed by a whale?

(Answer: Jonah)

NAMES FOUND IN THE BODY

Answer:

1.	Tropical trees.		Palms
2.	Weapons of war		Arms
3.	Bright flowers		Tulips
4.	Musical Instruments	(ear)	Drums
5.	A student		Pupil
6.	Used by Carpenters		Nails
7.	Part of a clock		Hands or face
8.	Large Box		Chest
9.	Strip of land		Neck
10.	Covers	(eye)	Lids

THOUGHT FOR THE MONTH:

"He who is slow to anger is better than the mighty, and
he who rules his spirit than he who takes a city."

Proverbs 16:32

HYMN: "I Would Be True" #361
SCRIPTURE: Galatians 5:22-6:6
MEDITATIVE THOUGHT: Self Control

Can the teacher who is impatient teach patience? Can the
parent who flies into ungovernable rages teach his child to be
even-tempered? Can the leader who is temperamental and ex-
citable teach his followers calm reason and rationalism? No
more can the Christian who lacks self-control teach others the
way to confidence in Christ, and peace of mind.

Only he who has complete control and mastery of himself and
his desires at all times can begin to have any control over the
events and circumstances surrounding his life. Perhaps that is
why we, in this atomic age, find it difficult to control the forces
of atomic power we have released in the world — because we
have not first learned to control ourselves.

We have wrongly come to associate the word "temperance"
with the idea of abstaining from drinking alcoholic beverages —
but temperance means so much more than that! It means tempering our thirst with self-control; tempering our appetites with
self-control: and tempering our bent to greediness with self-
control.

Let us strive to practice self-control to the end that we may
run with diligence the race that is set before us, for the prize of
the imperishable crown of eternal life. We are so prone in this
day to seek for ease and comfort, when we would do well to
cultivate the gospel of discipline — learning self-control, and
through this a better, safer, and more worthy control of our world
and the forces within it.

"Let him who is taught the word share all good things with
him who teaches" says our scripture for today. Let us be sure

that as a part of those good things we share, that we include the control of self — that we may seek first the Kingdom and find all needful things added unto us.

Let us bring forth the Christian virtue of self-control from its banishment and seclusion, and give it its rightful place among the fruits of the spirit.

PRAYER:

Almighty and understanding God, we come to Thee, earnestly seeking the power to control ourselves. Teach us to discipline our own desires that they may come into alignment with Thy Holy Will. Help us to so govern ourselves that we may be worthy to handle the power that is loosed in our hands in this atomic age. Make us truly followers of Thy Son, in being meek and lowly in heart. And bless us with the peace that comes as we accept Thy discipline and Thy rule. In Jesus' name we pray. Amen.

HYMN: "Jesus, I My Cross Have Taken" #375

BENEDICTION:

May we now repeat together the Mizpah benediction — "May the Lord watch between me and thee, while we are absent, one from the other. Amen."

SUGGESTIONS FOR THE HOSTESS

DECORATIONS:

Place a small (real) hatchet wrapped carefully in silver foil, in the center of the table. Cut small hatchets from red construction paper and place at random around the table. Use tall red candles. These small hatchets could be used as name cards, if so desired.

REFRESHMENTS:

Valley Forge Freeze, served with Lady Fingers, Hot chocolate and Coffee. Hard red cherry drops.

VALLEY FORGE FREEZE

1/2 Pint Whipping Cream (or 1/2 cup dry skim milk, whipped as directed on the package.)

3 Tablespoons Sugar

1 large bottle red Maraschino Cherries

17

Whip cream or milk till stiff. Add sugar gradually, whipping. Fold in the bottle of cherries and juice, and freeze in refrigerator trays set at the coldest, till frozen, then reduce cold to just keep frozen till needed. Cut in squares, and serve on plate with a lady finger at each side.

GAMES: Who Had This Vision?   Answer

1. A vision of four living creatures each having the face of a man, a lion, an ox and an eagle?

    1. Jeremiah, *Ezekiel,* Daniel

2. A vision of a great sheet let down from heaven on which were many creatures?

    2. James, Abraham, *Peter*

3. A vision of a man from a foreign land, crying "come over and help us?"

    3. Jacob, Joseph, *Paul*

4. A vision of a hand writing doom upon a palace wall?

    4. Sennacherib, *Belshazzar,* Nebuchadnezzar

5. A vision of a great city, with 12 gates, coming down to earth from heaven?

    5. Elisha, *John,* Elijah

Things George Washington Did Not Have

1. No coal, no wood, you need to burn
   To cook the meal to a brown turn.

    1. Electric or Gas range.

2. No pen, no pencil, no ancient quill,
   But you can write lots, if you will.

    2. Typewriter.

3. No need for brush, no need for broom,
   It's used a lot to clean the room.

    3. Vacuum Cleaner

4. You can talk to someone miles away,
   Whether or not you have much to say.

    4. Telephone

5. It keeps it hot, it keeps it cold,
   Whatever 'tis you make it hold.

   5. Thermos bottle

6. Its bright pencilled light illumines
      the way,
   A boon to the hiker who follows
      its ray.

   6. Flashlight

7. No iceman comes now to your
      door,
   But cold the food it keeps in store.

   7. Refrigerator

THOUGHT FOR THE MONTH:

"He will feed his flock like a shepherd, he will gather the lambs in his arms, he will carry them in his bosom, and gently lead those that are with young."

Isaiah 40:11

HYMN: "How Gentle God's Commands" #399

(To the tune Dennis — "Blest Be the Tie that Binds)

SCRIPTURE: James 3:6-18

MEDITATIVE THOUGHT: Gentleness

Even the very word "gentleness" has a subduing, quieting, soothing effect upon us. Yet gentleness is not be confused with weakness — "Gentle Jesus, meek and mild" we repeat, and we picture our Lord always as the kind of strong, manly yet gentle person that small children would never fear, but follow; never shun, but seek: never leave, but love.

Our word for man at his finest "gentleman" expresses no lack of strength. On the contrary, strength and gentleness are opposite words which nearly always go together.

When our eldest son was a tiny baby we had occasion to take a trip on a New York City subway — always noted for its rough, tough "take care of yourself, and never mind anyone else" philosophy. We reached the platform after all the train doors were shut and the train was about to pull out of the station. We sighed a little as we resigned ourselves to waiting for another train with a baby growing fretful.

To our amazement, the big burly motorman opened a door beside him, and motioned us to pass into the small cab where he sat to run the train, through an inner door into the train, and thus to take our places. The power of a tiny baby touched the heart of this great strong man to tenderness, and he determined that we should not have to wait on the subway platform for another train.

20

Gentleness may appear in every walk of life from the highest to the lowest of men — and we see it in the care of an animal for its young.

The gentleness of a doctor's touch that will not hurt, but heal; the gentleness of the preacher's words that seek not to break, but to bless; the gentleness of the parents' heart that yearns to supply the best in life to its child: — all these show forth the very nature of our Lord, for He was gentle, and meek, and lowly in heart, always.

PRAYER:

Dear Father of us all, wilt Thou teach us true Christian gentleness, that seeks to help and heal and bless where ever we may do so. Give us the strength of heart and mind and soul that makes for gentleness in our dealing with other people. Show us our own weaknesses, that we may be compassionate of the weakness of others. Teach us to be strong, that we may strengthen others — and to be gentle, that we may be an example of Christian love to all. For Jesus' sake we pray. Amen.

HYMN: "Jesus, The Very Thought of Thee #392

BENEDICTION:

"Bless us now as we close our devotional service — help us to serve Thee in all gentleness and humility, but with courage and hope in Thy ways — For our Lord's sake. Amen."

SUGGESTIONS FOR THE HOSTESS

DECORATIONS:

Cut two strips of orange crepe paper, 6 inches wide by 3 feet long: and one strip of dark green crepe paper the same size. Roll the papers tightly, then cut with scissors, 3 inch cuts close together on the paper, till it is like long paper fringe. Fasten the tightly rolled ends of the paper, each roll to a small stick. (lollypop sticks, swabsticks purchased at a drug store, or even pencils may be used.) Place three oranges on the table in a row. Insert the sticks with the orange paper on either side, and the dark green in the center orange. Fluff the paper fringe till you have

21

small plumes of crepe paper on top of your oranges. Use large orange candles with these.

REFRESHMENTS:

Serve orange sherbet with butter cake with orange icing. Make the icing with Confectioners Sugar and orange juice — grating the peel from half an orange into it, to add color and flavor. A few drops of lemon extract and orange food color will add to the beauty and taste of your cake. Have green mint patties and coffee with hot buttered nuts.

ORANGE SHERBET

Dissolve 1 1/2 cups of sugar in 2 cups boiling water. Add a package of orange gelatin, 2 cups cold water and 1 cup orange juice. Place in refrigerator tray and freeze to a heavy mush. Remove to a chilled bowl and beat till fluffy but not melted. Return to freezer and freeze till firm.

GAMES: Missing Object Search

Place small objects inconspicuously around room. Then give each player a list of the following descriptions. The player must find the object to fit each description, and write its name on the page.

Maid of Orleans	One molasses cookie
A letter from "home"	Letter O on a card
The Colonel	Kernel of corn
Our popular band	A rubber band
A perfect foot	Ruler
Headquarters	Hat or cap
The end of winter	Letter R on card
An old beau of mine	Ribbon bow
Where love is found	Dictionary
An absorbing article	Blotter

Famous Persons

What famous Bible characters do these things suggest?

1. A coat	Ans.	Joseph
2. A pillar of salt		Lot's wife
3. Mess of potage		Esau

22

4.	Whale	Jonah
5.	An apple	Eve
6.	Long hair	Samson
7.	Bulrushes	Moses
8.	Grain fields	Ruth
9.	Harp	David
10.	Ladder	Jacob

THOUGHT FOR THE MONTH:

"The grace which he gave us . . . . and now has manifested through the appearing of our Saviour Christ Jesus, who abolished death and brought life and immortality to light through the gospel."

"Timothy 1:9-10

HYMN: "Joyful, Joyful We Adore Thee"   #95

SCRIPTURE READING: Matthew 28:1-10

MEDITATIVE THOUGHT: Joy

Joy is one of the outstanding characteristics of the Christian religion. The two greatest days of the Christian year are both days of great joy: Christmas, the birthday of a Babe who was to change the course of history, and the hearts of men — and Easter, the dawning of man's immortal soul.

April is a most joyous time of year. It is as though nature were echoing the thought of resurrection. We feel surging within us resurrected hopes, resurrected dreams, resurrected opportunities for making our lives something worthy of the name "Christian."

The deep, abiding joy that pemeates the Christian religion and the Christian heart is based upon our assurance of eternal life. We who have that assurance as a birthright find it hard to realize how strange and wonderful it must have seemed to the early Christians, who accepted this new and amazing assurance of immortality with mixed emotions of fear and great joy! Suddenly, death no longer had dominion over the soul. The hopes that they harbored for immortality had become certainties! Their Lord, whom they feared dead, was alive again!

In the early days of the church, disciples of the "Way" greated each other with the words "He is risen!" to which the one so greeted responded, "He is risen, indeed!" Surely, such words could not be used in a faltering or half-hearted way. We know that they burst from lips that could not keep silence, because of the great joy within.

So may we, too, recapture some of that joy, felt so deeply by those early disciples; and may we see the eternal gate open on immortal dawn as we repeat, in tones as joyous as theirs — "He is risen, indeed!"

PRAYER:

Our Father in heaven, we pray that within our hearts may live the joy of Christianity, that we may understand, with all the saints of the church, the deep and abiding life that comes through serving Thee and Thy church. May we always remember that we serve a risen Lord, who walks beside us to guide us in the eternal way that leads to Thee. We pray in Jesus' name. Amen.

HYMN: "I Know That My Redeemer Liveth"   #255

BENEDICTION:

"Lord, wilt Thou bless us now and for all time. Amen."

SUGGESTIONS FOR THE HOSTESS

DECORATIONS:

White Easter lillies and/or white narcissus. White and red table candles.

REFRESHMENTS:

Spice cup cakes with white butter cream icing. Add red "sprinkles" or red cinnamon candy hearts for color. Vanilla ice cream with a teaspoon of red jelly on it. Jelly beans or spice drops, and coffee.

GAMES: Easter Bonnet

You will need a woman's old straw hat, (or a man's felt hat will do) and five pieces of white cardboard cut 2 1/2 by 4 1/2 inches. On these glue construction paper silhouettes — a bunny, an egg, a flower, a chick, and a candle. Place the hat in the center of the floor, upside down. Each person, in turn, flips the pieces of cardboard into the hat. Each piece that stays in the hat counts five points. The person with the most points, when all have flipped the cards, wins the game.

Famous People

(Match the name to the famous description.)

1. Methuselah	(7.) Raincoat
2. Solomon	(8.) Signature
3. Jezebel	(5.) Monster

25

4. Quizling
5. Frankenstein
6. Macadam
7. Macintosh
8. John Hancock

(6.) Pavement
(3.) Shameless woman
(1.) Very old man
(2.) Very wise man
(4.) Traitor

THOUGHT FOR THE MONTH:

> "The flowers appear on the earth, the time of singing
> has come, and the voice of the turtledove is heard in
> our land."   Song of Solomon 2:12

HYMN: "Come Thou Fount Of Every Blessing"   #111
SCRIPTURE READING: Psalm 96
MEDITATIVE THOUGHT: Praise

One of the favorite verses of a children's group I once led was from the Psalms: "Let the people praise thee, O God; let all the people praise thee!" (Psalm 67:3) They used to like to repeat it at roll call, or whenever a Bible verse was in order for any purpose.

It always comes back to my thoughts at this most beautiful time of the year, when trees are wearing bright new green garments, and the grass blades have a polished shine.

One of our most important tasks in this world is to praise God our Creator. We may praise Him with our minds, thinking, as we look on the glories of His creation, of the love and care with which He has made everything beautiful in its time. We may praise Him with our service, letting our hands be dedicated to the things that He would have them do to be a blessing to those around us. We may praise Him with our lips — lifting our own hearts and the hearts of others with our songs of praise.

Singing praise unto God is something that each one of us may do. We will not all be preachers, or even teachers or choir singers; but we can all add the honest adoration of our hearts in joyous song to God, our Creator, and Jesus Christ, our Saviour.

If we have an attitude of praise in our hearts, singing is almost a spontaneous expression of that attitude. God listens to the song in our hearts, not the tune on our lips!

Let us live in an attitude of praise to God for His mighty works, for His manifold blessings toward us. Let us praise Him with our minds, turning our thoughts to His creation when we see its beauty. Let us praise Him with our hands, finding ways

27

in which we may serve Him, in His church, and serve others of His children. Let us praise Him with our voices — for He has done marvelous things for us all!

PRAYER:

Our Father, make us ever mindful of the wonder, the glory and the beauty of Thy creation. Open our eyes to see the beauty, our ears to hear the song, and our minds and lips to think and speak Thy praise! All Thy creation seems to be singing praise to Thee at this time of the year, in the glory of new spring beauty. May we, Thy highest creation, join in the chorus of praise to our Maker, our God, and our Redeemer. In the name of our Lord, Jesus Christ, we pray. Amen.

HYMN: "Lead On, O King Eternal"   #363

BENEDICTION:

". . . . . . . Amen! Blessing and glory and wisdom and thanksgiving and honor and power and might be to our God for ever and ever. Amen." Revelation 7:12

SUGGESTIONS FOR THE HOSTESS

DECORATIONS:

Forsythia and daffodils — tall yellow candles. Yellow and white candy mints in small dishes at each end of table.

REFRESHMENTS:

Sliced peaches with whipped cream (or plain). Lay a lace paper doily on top of a still slightly warm large cake (butter cake or spongecake, as preferred). Dust confectioners sugar on top of the doily so that it leaves a lacy pattern on the cake, before cutting into squares for serving.

GAMES: Windy Words

Divide into two groups. Designate one person from each group to write down suggestions. Allow one minute for the groups to remember and write down as many words as they can relating to winds. (Suggested words — breeze, gust, gale, roar, cyclone, squall, whiff, puff, etc.)

Which One?

(Check which is correct.)

1. A cousin of Saul, and commander of Saul's Army
   Abner   X
   Ahab

2. The home of Mary, Martha and Lazarus
   Bethel
   Bethany   X

3. One to whom Jesus appeared on the Emmaus road
   Cornelius
   Cleopas   X

4. A silver coin used by the Romans
   Denarius   X
   Demetrius

5. One who cared for young Samuel
   Eli   X
   Elisha

THOUGHT FOR THE MONTH:

"Fight the good fight of faith; take hold of the eternal life to which you were called when you made the good confession in the presence of many witnesses."

I Timothy 6:12

HYMN: "Are Ye Able?" #360

SCRIPTURE READING: Hebrews 11:1-10

MEDITATIVE THOUGHT: Faith

"We live by faith, not by sight" — how very true this is of our whole lives, even in the material world. Every time we catch a train or a plane, every time we set our clocks by radio time, every time we touch a light switch and wait confidently for the resulting flood of light — we are acting in faith.

Our scientists and mathematicians count always on the inflexibility of the natural laws in our universe — that is their starting point for any hypothesis. We know that God has set these natural laws in our world to control it and keep it running in an orderly fashion. How we take for granted such simple things as that two and two will always be four! Our God intervenes or changes natural law so seldom in our universe that when He does, we call it miracle!

How strange that any could have faith in the rules of creation, and be weak in faith in the Creator! He who is great enough to have created this vast universe with its many laws, is also great enough to govern and bring it, through His purposes, to the destiny for which He intended it!

God has a purpose for His universe, and a purpose for each one of us, if we accept and fulfill that purpose. Faith is putting our trust in God, sure that He can accomplish, with our weak help, the things which we could never achieve for Him alone! It is not doubting, though clouds of sorrow obscure the sun, that beyond the clouds, God's sun of joy is shining: it is not doubting, though for a while wrong seems to triumph, that right will be the ultimate victor in our world, under God. Faith is the perfect trust in God that the martyrs achieved. Not belief that He will remove from our lives all pain, all illness, all sorrow, or even death. But that by holding tightly to His Hand, we may go through any of these tests, and emerge as Christian victors — confident that all things work together for good, to those that love the Lord.

PRAYER:

Almighty God and Everlasting Father, wilt Thou strengthen our faith in Thee, that we may walk in perfect trust that Thou art with us and wilt guide and protect us throughout all of life: and when we take the great step from our world of the flesh into Thy world of the spirit, wilt Thou hold our hand, that we may not falter, or faint, but come to Thee in blessed assurance. Bless us now and keep us as we strive to do Thy Will. In Jesus' name. Amen.

HYMN: "My Faith Looks Up To Thee"   #355

BENEDICTION:

Peace be to the brethren, and love with faith, from God the Father and the Lord Jesus Christ. Grace be with all who love our Lord Jesus Christ with love undying. Amen. Ephesians 6:23

SUGGESTIONS FOR THE HOSTESS

DECORATIONS:

Place narrow blue crepe paper streamers from the centerpiece to the edge of the table. Pin pink "wedding bells" cut from pink construction paper a foot apart on the streamers. Use blue and pink tall candles. The small celluloid dolls may be dressed as bride and groom for the center of the table, if something more elaborate is desired.

REFRESHMENTS:

Vanilla ice cream with frozen or fresh sliced strawberries. Plain sugar cookies or vanilla wafers. Pillow mints in assorted pastel colors. Choice of hot coffee or iced tea.

GAMES: Question The Quotes

If the following quotations are from the Bible, mark B, if from other source, Mark O.

1. "A good name is rather to be chosen than riches."　　1. B
2. "To thine own self be true, and it must follow, as the night the day, thou canst not then be false to any man."　　2. O
3. "Life is real, life is earnest, and the grave is not its goal."　　3. O
4. "A wise son heareth his father's instruction"　　4. B
5. "Faith is the substance of things hoped for"　　5. B
6. "A rose, by any other name, would smell as sweet"　　6. O

Name The Tree

		Answer
1. What tree is prone to languish and sigh?	1.	Pine
2. What tree is found only after a fire?	2.	Ash
3. What tree is used around the neck?	3.	Fir
4. What tree is the neatest tree?	4.	Spruce
5. What tree is carried in the hand?	5.	Palm
6. What tree grows by sea and lake?	6.	Beech

THOUGHT FOR THE MONTH:

"Moreover it is required of stewards that they be found
trustworthy . . . ."   1 Corinthians 4:2

HYMN: "God Send Us Men"   #377

SCRIPTURE READING: Luke 16:1-13

MEDITATIVE THOUGHT: Loyalty

Perhaps we are more aware of the need for loyalty to the
church during the warm summer months than at any other time
during the year. The ordinary routine of the year is often dis-
rupted by vacations and trips. The children are home from
school, and there is much extra work to be done, both in the
city and in the country. Many times our classes and class meetings are small during the summer. So let us try to make up in
enthusiasm for the lack in numbers!

Surely the loyalty of God's people is an important thing at all
times. Let us strive for loyal support of the efforts of the church
throughout the year.

Let us remember that our stewardship is strained most during
vacation times — but so is the budget of the church! The ex-
penses of the church go on; but sometimes, when we are away
on Sundays, we forget that our gifts, whether large or small, will
be missed.

If we are in strange communities during the summer, let us
be sure to find a church where we may worship with other Christians. Our very presence in that "vacation" church may be the
encouragement that they need to help them carry on in fellowship. Surely, our loyalty to our own local church will be deep-
ened by this fellowship with other Christians while we are away
from home.

Jesus said: "Make friends for yourself by means of unrighteous
mammon," and we would determine now, today, to make friends
for the Kingdom of God by our faithful and loyal attendance and
gifts at His worship service, wherever we may be.

PRAYER:

Gracious Father, we come to Thee this day, asking that Thou wilt bless our hearts with a sense of loyalty to Thy Word, to Thy church and to Thy work. May we endeavor to live our lives in loyalty to the ideals taught us by Thy Son, Jesus, for in His name we pray. Amen.

HYMN: "I Would Be True" #361

BENEDICTION:

"Whatsoever we do in word and deed, may it be done in the name of the Lord Jesus, giving thanks to God the Father by Him. Amen."

SUGGESTIONS FOR THE HOSTESS

DECORATIONS:

A low center bowl of red roses, together with their leaves, and either floating red flower candles in small bowls at either end, or low red candles in holders.

REFRESHMENTS:

Cherry pie with wedges of golden American cheese. Vanilla ice cream or whipped cream, or a dusting of confectioners sugar may be added for beauty. Hard red candy balls and buttered nuts, and Coffee.

GAMES: What To Wear On Vacation

	Answer
1. The artist?	1. Canvas
2. The editor?	2. Prints
3. The banker?	3. Checks
4. The hunter?	4. Duck
5. The government official?	5. Red tape
6. The gas station attendant?	6. "Oil" cloth
7. The fisherman?	7. Net
8. The prisoner?	8. Stripes
9. The dairyman?	9. Cheesecloth
10. The gardener?	10. Lawn

These clues should be read one at a time, with a pause for thinking. The first person to guess the woman's identity wins the game.

A. My daughter was married to one of the Apostles.

B. One day I became very ill when Jesus was expected.

C. Jesus saw me lying down and knew I had a fever.

D. He touched my hand, and the fever left me immediately.

E. I was able to get up and perform my duties as hostess.

WHO AM I?   (Answer: Peter's wife's mother)

THOUGHT FOR THE MONTH:

"Take your share of suffering as a good soldier of
Christ Jesus."   2 Timothy 2:3

HYMN: "O Master, Let Me Walk With Thee"   #307

SCRIPTURE READING: Romans 2:1-11

MEDITATIVE THOUGHT: Endurance

"But he who endures to the end shall be saved," said Jesus in
the twenty-fourth chapter of Matthew's Gospel. There are many
times in life when the power to endure is one that we greatly
need, and often greatly lack.

We frequently speak of "enduring" the heat of the summer,
or the cold of the winter. I wonder, however, if we do not do
the word an injustice, for to "endure" has a much deeper meaning than these small inconveniences.

Endurance is a quality that the Christian needs when he is
faced with pain or sorrow, and being a Christian does not re-
lease him from the threat of these trials. Who among us can go
through life without meeting these deep things of the spirit? Let
us cultivate the ability to endure, through the grace of our Lord,
and by His srength, so that we may truly inherit more abundant
and more meaningful life.

May our endurance not be of the negative type which bows
its head in defeat, but rather that inner strength which allows
us to meet whatever life may bring with the conscious knowledge
that God is with us, and that "underneath are the everlasting
arms."

The patient endurance that is based on calm, inner strength
can resist every trial and emerge victorious, right to the end.

He who endures through trial and pain,

Finds there is always something to gain;

He who walks calmly the way of woe,

Clings close to the Saviour's love, we know.

PRAYER:

Father in heaven, wilt Thou teach us how to endure patiently those trials which come to us. Help us to grow in strength as we try to walk in Thy light, following the path that leads us toward eternal day. Bless our fellowship together, that we may strengthen one another in Thy way — In Jesus' name we pray, Amen.

HYMN: "The Lord Is My Shepherd" #170

BENEDICTION: (Repeated in unison)

May the Lord watch between thee and me, while we are absent, one from the other. In Jesus' name, Amen.

SUGGESTIONS FOR THE HOSTESS

DECORATIONS:

Purple and pink flowers, — asters, bachelor buttons or petunias. Pink tall candles.

REFRESHMENTS:

Fruit salad molded in grape or black raspberry Jello, served on lettuce leaves, with sugar cookies and pink and white mints. Iced tea, or soft drinks.

GAMES: The Seven Seas

The word which answers each definition is one ending in the sound "sea". (The answers, given correctly here, should be scrambled if used as a written game.)

		Answer
1. What sea is very cold?		1. Icy
2. What sea is a fowl stewed in gravy?		2. Fricassee
3. What sea is an imaginary tale?		3. Fantasy
4. What sea is a pressing need?		4. Urgency
5. What sea is extreme delight?		5. Ecstasy
6. What sea is empty?		6. Vacancy
7. What sea is proper?		7. Decency
8. What sea is a sudden need?		8. Emergency
9. What sea is faithful?		9. Constancy
10. What sea is highly decorated?		10. Fancy

Who Were These Bible Dreamers?

Match the names to the descriptions. (If written, scramble the answers)

1. His dreams so angered his brothers that they plotted against him.   Joseph — Genesis 37
2. He saw a ladder reaching up to heaven, and angels going up and down.   Jacob — Genesis 28:12
3. He dreamed that seven lean cows ate up seven fat cows.
                                    Pharaoh — Genesis 41
4. He dreamed that God said to him, "Ask what I shall give you." He asked for wisdom.   Solomon — 1 Kings 3
5. He dreamed that an angel warned him to take his wife and young child and flee to Egypt.   Joseph — Matthew 2:13

". . . . if any of you lacks wisdom, let him ask of God, who gives to all men generously and without reproaching, and it will be given him."　　　　James 1:5

HYMN: "God, Who Madest Earth And Heaven"　＃143
SCRIPTURE READING: 1 Corinthians 1: 17-27
MEDITATIVE THOUGHT: Wisdom

Man has been, for ages, on a never-ending search for wisdom. Yet with all his wisdom, he must also find understanding and insight, or his wisdom will avail him very little.

We may find the way to explode the atom; but unless we also learn how to control it and harness it for the good of mankind, we gain little because of our knowledge of this immeasurable force.

We know from history that a man may be very wise in the ways of the world, yet miss finding happiness, or the deeper, more important things of the spirit.

Solomon asked God for wisdom, and wisdom was granted him — but a man with keener vision has said, "The beginning of wisdom is this: Get wisdom, and whatever you get, get insight." (Prov. 4:7)

We spend many years of our lives acquiring an education, that our minds may be rich in knowledge — but if we neglect to use our learning for bettering our own lives and the lives of those we love, education may become a worthless thing to us. The wisdom of this world may be foolishness to God, and the wisdom of God may seem foolishness to those who are worldly minded.

The teachings of Jesus ". . . . . turn the other cheek . . .!" ". . . . . . love your enemies . . ." " . . . bless them that curse you . . . ." " . . . give to everyone that asks of you . . ." — may seem foolish to the worldly man, and impossible to do. Yet this is the way to abundant life! Insofar as we follow His teachings, we achieve life that is richer, fuller, and more satisfying.

"Get wisdom; get insight. Do not forsake her, and she will keep you; love her, and she will guard you."

PRAYER:

Father, wilt Thou help us to be wise, not in the ways of the world, but in the things of the spirit. Help us to grow in knowledge and in understanding, that we may use whatever talents and abilities we may possess in Thy service. So teach us to number our days that we may apply our hearts unto wisdom — in Thy dear Son's name. Amen.

HYMN: "How Firm A Foundation" #406

BENEDICTION:

Our Father, please bless us now as we go to our homes, that we may be a blessing to those we love. In Jesus' name we ask it. Amen.

SUGGESTIONS FOR THE HOSTESS

DECORATIONS:

Scarlet and gold zinnias in a bowl, and scarlet and gold (or yellow) candles. Bright red and gold autumn leaves may be added to this if available.

REFRESHMENTS:

Fruit salad, made with a variety of colorful fruits, and New England Cream Cake.

Cream 1/4 cup shortening with 1 cup sugar. Add beaten egg and 1 tsp. vanilla. Sift together 1 and 2/3 cups flour, 2 tsps. baking powder, and 1/4 tsp. salt. Add alternately with 1/2 cup milk to creamed mixture. Bake at 350 degrees about 25 minutes in layer cake pans. Put together with cooked cream filling. Scald 1 cup milk in top of double boiler. Add 1 egg beaten with 6 tblsp. sugar, 4 tblsp. flour, dash of salt and 1/2 tsp. vanilla. Cook till mixture thickens. Cool before spreading between layers of cake. Dust top of cake with confectioners sugar, and serve with coffee or iced tea.

Nature Quiz

(Answers should be scrambled, if written)

1. Which runs faster, a greyhound or whippet?	1. Whippet
2. What animal carries its home on its back, and has its eyes in its horns?	2. Snail
3. Do fleas have wings?	3. No, they hop
4. Which of these is the largest, lion, tiger or jaguar?	4. Tiger
5. What have the cougar, panther, puma and mountain lion in common?	5. In America, all are the same.

Relationships In The Bible

1. Abraham and Lot	4. Husband and Wife
2. David and Absolom	1. Uncle and Nephew
3. Ruth and Naomi	5. Cousins
4. Aquila and Priscilla	2. Father and Son
5. Mary and Elizabeth	3. Mother-in-law, Daughter-in-law
6. Jacob and Esau	7. Brother — Sister
7. Lazarus and Mary	6. Brothers

THOUGHT FOR THE MONTH:

". . . . we exhort you, brethren, admonish the idle, encourage the faint-hearted, help the weak, be patient
with them all."   I Thessalonians 5:14

HYMN: "God Of Our Fathers" #551

SCRIPTURE READING: Isaiah 35:1-10

MEDITATIVE THOUGHT: Courage

Christian courage is a quality that is quite different from what
the world often acclaims as courage. It has nothing to do with
physical size or health, but is a quality of the spirit, rather than
a thing of the flesh. It is a quality of soul that any Christian may
achieve, no matter their size or physical condition or place in life.
This kind of courage may only be obtained through prayer and
trust in God, and quiet communion with Him.

It is the sort of quiet strength that, relying on a loving Father,
can face disappointment, pain, or tragic loss, and rise above them
to find purpose and meaning in life because God still rules, and
serving Him and striving to grow in Christianity make life worth
living.

Christian courage makes a mother a tower of strength in a
child's fatal illness: or keeps a father steady and sure in adversity
or poverty.

We are so apt to think of courage in this world's terms —
something to be associated with physical strength; with drums
rolling and flags flying — yet even in wartime, the greatest courage may be displayed in the quiet way a person bears pain or
affliction, rather than on the battlefield!

> This is my prayer: —
>
>   To look on life with quiet eyes,
>   And know, when sorrow veils our skies:
>   Beyond the mourning and the tears,
>   Beyond the dreary march of years —
>   Lies God's sunrise!

PRAYER:

Dear God, source of all strength and courage for the Christian, wilt Thou touch our hearts with Thy peace, and give us the calm trust that only Thou canst give. Teach us through prayer and communion with Thee to gain the strength and Christian courage that shall carry us through all the trials, and sorrows, and temptations of this life: that we may at last attain to that greater, brighter life. In Jesus' name we pray. Amen.

HYMN: "Beneath The Cross Of Jesus" #235

BENEDICTION:

Our Father, wilt Thou bless us with quietness and peace, and give us strength to carry on in Thy Son's name, for in His name we ask it. Amen.

SUGGESTIONS FOR THE HOSTESS

DECORATIONS:

Brown or green candles. Brown and green autumn leaves. If real leaves are unavailable, brown and green construction paper leaves may be made and used.

REFRESHMENTS:

Cider or apple juice and glazed doughnuts make a delicious and seasonal snack, and mixed warm buttered nuts add to the festivity.

GAMES: In This Place

Each answer is the name of a place. Mix them when making list.

1. David's boyhood home	1. Bethlehem
2. Where Noah's Ark grounded	2. Ararat
3. Garden where Jesus prayed	3. Gethsemane
4. Joseph worked as a carpenter here	4. Nazareth
5. Paul came here after he was converted	5. Damascus
6. Peter and Andrew fished in this sea	6. Galilee

43

7. Lot fled from this city	7. Sodom
8. David met Goliath here	8. Elah
9. John was exiled here	9. Patmos
10. Jesus was baptized here	10. Jordan River

Halloween Faces

Each guest should be given a large paper bag and crayons. Each tears holes for eyes, nose and mouth, and draws some funny face on the bag. All place the bags over their heads, and become a room full of Halloween characters. A small prize might be given for the funniest face.

THOUGHT FOR THE MONTH:

>"Enter into his gates with thanksgiving, and his courts
>with praise! Give thanks to him, bless his name! For
>the Lord is good; . . . . ."   Psalm 100:4-5a

HYMN: "All Hail The Power" #252

SCRIPTURE READING: Ephesians 5:11-20

MEDITATIVE THOUGHT: Thankfulness

During this month, which includes the national day of Thanksgiving, it seems good for us to consider for a little while the importance of the grace of gratitude — and the rarity of its expression.

In our Bible we read a story that tells of Jesus' healing of ten lepers. Of these ten, nine were so delighted that they left immediately, without a thought of thanks. Only one returned to express his thanks and undying devotion to the One who had helped him. One in ten with the grace of gratitude! That is a mighty small percentage, yet I wonder if it doesn't portray our own lack?

Once a man climbed to the topmost peak of the roof to hunt for a leak in his home. At last he found the break in the roofing, managed to seal it to his satisfaction and started to climb down toward the tall ladder that leaned against the side of the house. Then he lost his footing!

For a long, terrible minute he fought frantically to stop his slide toward the edge of the roof. Although it had been a long time since he had sought the presence of God, he found himself praying:

>"O Lord, if you'll only save me from this terrible fall,
>I'll promise to live a better life. Lord, I'm asking You
>for a miracle — save me!"

And then his heavy cord trousers caught on a protruding nail. There was a harsh, ripping sound, but they caught and held! The man drew a long breath of relief, cautiously edging his way to the ladder, and lifted his voice to God again.

45

"Never mind, Lord," he said cheerfully, "I caught on a nail!"

How many times, like that man, do we refuse to recognize God's miracles because they involve the use of some insignificant means — like a nail! A truly thankful heart is one of the things that shows we are a child of God. Let us resolve to be — always — the one in ten who returns to give thanks!

PRAYER:

Loving Heavenly Father, wilt Thou grant to us the blessing of grateful hearts? May our souls overflow with love and thankfulness for Thy many blessings and kindnesses toward us. And may we never fail to understand that Thou mightest use the very humblest instrument to work miracles in our lives. In the name of Thy Son Jesus we pray. Amen.

HYMN: "Come Ye Thankful People Come" #593

BENEDICTION:

Now, O Father, send us to our several homes bearing in our hearts the grace of gratitude. May we see and be thankful for Thy great bounty and blessings to us. In Jesus' name. Amen.

SUGGESTIONS FOR THE HOSTESS

DECORATIONS:

Orange or flame colored candles. A centerpiece of polished fruits, whatever is locally available, with trailing bits of ivy vines.

REFRESHMENTS:

Small sandwiches of peanut butter on fancy crackers. Colored mint patties. Individual pumpkin pies made in tart shells, or pieces of pumpkin pie with whipped cream. Coffee.

GAMES: Whom Do These Suggest?

1. A dish of venison?	Answers:	1. Jacob
2. A bush on fire?		2. Moses
3. Gold, Frankincense, Myrrh?		3. Jesus
4. A rooster crowing?		4. Peter
5. A large fish?		5. Jonah

6. A fiery furnace?

7. A lion's den?
8. A huge boat?
9. A coat of many colors?
10. A chariot of fire?

6. Shadrach,
Meshack,
Abednego
7. Daniel
8. Noah
9. Joseph
10. Elijah

Thanks

Write the word "THANKS" on small cards, one letter on each card. Give one letter to each guest as they arrive — striving to be sure they are given out in groups of six so that words may be formed. Guests try to discover other guests with letters to spell out the word "thanks". They link arms with those holding the letter immediately preceding or following their own letter, till six guests have spelled out the word THANKS. Wait till all the groups have discovered their matching letters before ending the game.

THOUGHT FOR THE MONTH:

"For to us a child is born, to us a son is given; and the government will be upon his shoulder and his name will be called 'Wonderful Counselor, Mighty God, Everlasting Father, Prince of Peace.' " — Isaiah 9:6

HYMN: "Silent Night, Holy Night" #188

SCRIPTURE READING: Hebrews 6:9-19

MEDITATIVE THOUGHT: Hope

"Unto us a child is born." What moment in the life of an individual is more filled with hope than that moment when a child is born? The hope of nations rests in the hands of new-born babes, who will grow up to be the leaders of tomorrow!

Who does not breathe a prayer that the tiny baby we cradle in our arms may someday become a force for good in our world? How natural that God should have chosen a baby to be the light of the world, the hope of the world, and the Saviour of the world!

How Mary's heart must have thrilled within her as she held her dear baby close in her arms on that holy night so long ago! This is a month of warm and tender memories, as we call to mind again the birth of Jesus, our eternal Hope.

May we be filled anew with the glorious hope of Christmas as we remember the birthday of our Lord with joy in our hearts.

Rays of joy and hope and love have shone down through the centuries to brighten our lives. May we rejoice anew, in the glorious news of the birth of our Saviour, Jesus Christ, the hope of the world — who came to bring peace to the hearts of men!

PRAYER:

Our Father, and Father of all living beings, wilt Thou make us more surely aware of Thy love and care at this most wonderful season of the year. Help us to recapture the wonder of that joy and hope contained in a small stable so long ago. May our hearts overflow with love for all Thy creatures during this joyous season, and may the spirit of Christmas be carried in our hearts all through the year — long after the glow of the season has faded away around us. Bless and keep us and make us truly Thine is our prayer in Jesus' name. Amen.

HYMN: "Hark! The Herald Angels Sing" #189

BENEDICTION:

May the words of our mouths and the meditations of our hearts be acceptable in Thy sight, O Lord, our strength and our Redeemer. For Jesus' sake. Amen.

SUGGESTIONS FOR THE HOSTESS

DECORATIONS:

A small plastic table tree decorated with vari-colored spice drops or a tiny live evergreen tree with small real ornaments will be very pretty. Christmas candles in fancy shapes may be added.

REFRESHMENTS:

Lime Jello, cut with a Christmas tree cookie cutter. Put bits of maraschino cherries at the tip of each "branch" as ornaments, and decorate with ribbons of colored whipped cream or icing, forced through a cake decorator. With this serve plain cake, colored mint patties, coffee and hot spiced tea.

GAMES: Number Please!

(Choose the correct number)

1. During the great flood it rained	400	<u>40</u>	10	days
2. How many people entered the Ark?	6	<u>8</u>	12	
3. The Israelites wandered in the wilderness	<u>40</u>	80	300	years
4. How old was Abraham when Isaac was born?	120	90	<u>100</u>	years
5. How old was Methuselah?	999	987	<u>969</u>	years
6. When Hezekiah was dying, how many years did God add to his life?	<u>15</u>	6	9	

7. How many Hebrew children were cast into the fiery furnace?   4   5   <u>3</u>

8. How many disciples did Jesus choose?   11   120   <u>12</u>

9. How many sons did Jacob have?   2   <u>12</u>   16

10. Jesus was tempted in the wilderness —   20   <u>40</u>   30 days

THOUGHT FOR THE MONTH:

> "Let not your hearts be troubled; believe in God, believe also in me. In my Father's house are many rooms; if it were not so, would I have told you that I go to prepare a place for you?"   John 14:1-2

HYMN: "Nearer, My God, To Thee."   #329

SCRIPTURE READING: 2 Corinthians 3: 4-18

MEDITATIVE THOUGHT: Trust

"Though He slay me, yet will I trust Him." This was the cry of Job (13:15) and we would echo his great words of faith and confidence.

"Trust in the Lord with all thine heart, and lean not unto thine own understanding," said the writer of the Book of Proverbs (3:5). We find his words of assurance as applicable to our day as to his.

We sing often of our "blessed assurance" without stopping to wonder if we truly have that assurance. We need trust and faith in times of trouble, pain and difficulty.

Real trust in God touches the deep springs of the soul and drinks freely of the water of life offered to us by our Lord and Master, Jesus Christ.

It is the kind of trust that lets a small child walk through danger or darkness fearlessly, if he can hold tightly to a loved one's hand.

If we could draw near enough to our heavenly Father to reach out in faith and slip our hand confidently into His, we, too, could walk through danger, or pain, or darkness, or trouble, buoyed up by the confidence that we are not alone, but have a loving Father who cares and goes with us through the darkness of this world.

> "Trust in the Lord", Proverbs tell us, and we respond — We will trust in the Lord — though He slay us, yet will we trust Him, for life and death are in His loving, gentle hands."

PRAYER:

Dear heavenly Father, who hast led us so gently down the

long and sometimes arduous trails of this life, we bless Thee for Thy tender care for us, and we ask that Thou wilt continue to walk with us, guiding and protecting us from evil, and that we may appear in Thy sight worthy of eternal life. For these blessings we pray, that our trust may become deeper and our faith firmer. In Jesus' name. Amen.

HYMN: "Blessed Assurance" #412

BENEDICTION:

May the peace of God and the assurance and faith of our Lord Jesus Christ, bless our lives from this time forth and even for evermore. Amen.

SUGGESTIONS FOR THE HOSTESS

DECORATIONS:

A small plastic tree may be trimmed with red spice drops, or red heart-shaped gumdrops. Tall red candles at either end.

REFRESHMENTS:

Home-made cookies cut with heart shaped cookie cutter, and sprinkled with red sugar, or iced with pink icing; Pink tinted fruit punch and mixed nuts.

GAMES: Old Or New Testament?

		Answers —
1. Psalms	1. O. T.
2. The Beatitudes	2. N. T.
3. Four Gospels	3. N. T.
4. The Ten Commandments	4. O. T.
5. The Sermon on the Mount	5. N. T.
6. Paul's Epistles	6. N. T.
7. Ruth and Boaz	7. O. T.
8. David and Jonathan	8. O. T.
9. Book of Acts	9. N. T.
10. Journey to Promised Land	10. O. T.
11. Story of Job	11. O. T.
12. Journeys of Paul	12. N. T.

End These Similes

Try to invent your own definitions and let the group decide whether or not the answer is acceptable. A few suggested similes are listed as answers, but any descriptive term will do.

1. As big as	A barn
2. As pretty as	A picture
3. As old as	Methuselah
4. As young as	A minute
5. As new as	A new penny
6. As ugly as	A bulldog
7. As fierce as	A bear
8. As cunning as	A fox
9. As sharp as	A knife
10. As tall as	A mountain

SUPPLEMENT PROGRAM NO. 2   THEME — GROWTH

THOUGHT FOR THE MONTH:

"Rather, speaking the truth in love, we are to grow up
in every way into him who is the head, into Christ."

Ephesians 4:15

HYMN: "Lord, Speak To Me"   #470
SCRIPTURE READING: 2 Peter 1:3-11
MEDITATIVE THOUGHT: Growth

I had a strange and wonderful dream last night. I dreamed
that I stood at the beautiful gate of heaven, and glory shone all
around, a glory that was more than sunshine.

I felt very humble as I looked around me, for I was surrounded
by a great and distinguished-looking company. Next to me stood
a beautiful blonde woman, with pale, white, unblemished skin
and blue eyes, and a grace of movement that made me feel very
old and awkward. Beyond her stood an old and stooped Negro
man with frizzy grey hair and an attitude of self-effacement.

A tall bronzed young man stood proudly, with rippling muscles
in shoulders and back bespeaking the completely fit athlete. With
shoulders bent was a scholarly man, who even now looked to be
peering into a printed page, although he held no book.

In a corner was a small, mousy woman, who looked as if she
would be afraid to utter a word. Oh, it was a motley group who
stood waiting for admittance at the gate of heaven!

Then suddenly, the Lord was there before us, and the glory of the Lord shone round about us, and I was sore afraid — and the Lord said —

"How well have you done about growing a soul?" I knew that He was talking to each one of us; and though His voice was gentle and compassionate, I winced.

"I have kept myself untouched by the ugliness of the world," the pale blonde white woman said; "I am pure white and clean — "

The Lord smiled, but it was a pitying smile, and He turned to the grey-haired Negro —

"Have you grown a soul?" He asked —

"I have tried — " the old man said humbly, and wept as the Lord motioned him on through the gate.

"I have kept myself strong and clean, and untouched by grief or pain" the young athlete said proudly "Have I not grown — "

Again the Lord smiled in pity.

"Tell me not the color of your skin — but the depth of your soul," He said. "Tell me not the size of your muscles, but the size of your love for God and man. Tell me not of the greatness of your intellect, but of the greatness of your compassion for human need." Then He turned, and seemed to look directly at me.

"Go back! You have one more chance," he said. "But this time, grow a soul!"

I woke to the knowledge that I should be about the biggest task in the universe — the growing of a human soul worthy to enter the garden of God!

PRAYER:

Dear God, help us to grow souls that are worthy. Help us to pride ourselves, not in the color of our skins, or in our possessions, or even in the greatness of our minds, but in the growth of our souls, which is the reason for Thy placing us in this world. In Jesus' name we pray, and with His help we shall grow. Amen.

HYMN: "My Life, My Love, I Give To Thee"   #293

BENEDICTION:

Grow in grace and knowledge of our Lord and Saviour, Jesus

Christ. To Him be glory both now and to the day of eternity. Amen. (2 Peter 3:18)

SUGGESTIONS FOR THE HOSTESS

DECORATIONS:

Use long sprays of yellow forsythia to carry out a yellow and green motif. Put green and yellow candles on each side of the forsythia. Use narrow strips of green and yellow crepe paper streamers from the center of the table to the edges.

REFRESHMENTS:

Serve spice cup cakes with green confectioners sugar icing; buttered nuts and Wheat Chex (recipe on the box) and coffee and green candy mint leaves and yellow mint patties. Place carefully on the plates so that they look like flowers with leaves.

GAMES: Brain Twisters

(Do not use paper and pencil for these)

What is the one-syllable word appearing in the Bible whose pronounciation is changed when the first letter is capitalized?

Answer: job — Job

Name a four letter word in English ending in eny?

Answer: deny

Shout It Out

Send one person out of the room. While he is out, the group decides on the title of a hymn. Each person is given a word of the title till each person has a word. When the person who is "it" comes back, all shout their words at the same time. Then the person who is "it" may ask one question of each person. In the answer, each person must use his particular "word" in some way.

SUPPLEMENTAL PROGRAM NO. 3   THEME — SONG

THOUGHT FOR THE MONTH:

"Then shall the lame man leap like a hart, and the tongue of the dumb sing for joy. For waters shall break forth in the wilderness, and streams in the desert."

Isaiah 35:6

HYMN: "When Morning Gilds The Skies" #135
SCRIPTURE READING: Ephesians 5: 6-20
MEDITATIVE THOUGHT: Song

Too seldom do we think of song as an essential part of our worship of God — and an essential part of life. Yet every person has a tendency to burst into song or some sort of tune at happy moments of life. It is so often a spontaneous act of worship or thanksgiving, even unspoken, for the blessings of life.

Many ministers have been disturbed at the insincere way in which Christians sing words that have deep and lofty meanings. We who abhor insincerity, can still sing phrases of hymns which, if we truly lived up to them, would change our whole lives.

When I was junior age in Sunday School I found it very difficult to sing the words of one verse of a hymn. The words were "But thousands and thousands who wander and fall — never heard of the heavenly home. How I wish they could know there is room for them all, and that Jesus has bid them to come."

In my childish mind it seemed wrong to sing "How I wish they could know," since I was not planning to be a missionary. "If I *truly* wished that they could know," I reasoned "I'd have to *do* something about it."

Perhaps the sincerity of a child was one of the things that Jesus meant when He said "Unless you turn and become like children, you will never enter the kingdom of heaven." Matthew 18:3

Let our songs be sung with more sincerity. Let us echo the words of our great hymn poets, as if we, too, meant every word. Then indeed will our singing become true worship and the music of the church will become a part of the worship of our God.

May we come into His presence with singing, but let us sing with meaning and sincerity. Let us truly worship with our songs!

PRAYER:

Our God and Father, our hearts would sing joyous praise of Thy great goodness toward us. We bless Thee for Thy many kindnesses; and we come with thankful hearts, for the great blessings of Thy word, and Thy grace toward us. Bless and keep us now and forever. We ask in Jesus' name. Amen.

HYMN: "Sing Them Over Again To Me" #442

BENEDICTION:

The grace of the Lord Jesus Christ and the love of God and the fellowship of the Holy Spirit be with you all. Amen. (2 Corinthians 13:14)

SUGGESTIONS FOR THE HOSTESS

DECORATIONS:

Fill a low bowl with French marigolds in yellow and brown, or with black-eyed susans. Use yellow and brown streamers of crepe paper for additional color for the table, if desired, and yellow candles in low holders.

REFRESHMENTS:

Serve squares of lemon fluff, with coffee and burnt sugar peanuts.

Lemon Fluff — 1 pkg. lemon Jello, 1 cup boiling water, 1 cup sugar, 1 tblsp. lemon juice, 1 tall can evaporated milk, chilled and whipped stiff. 14 Graham crackers, crushed into crumbs.

Mix Jello, water, sugar and lemon juice, and cool till syrupy. Line large pan or casserole with half the graham cracker crumbs. Pour Jello mixture into whipped evaporated milk, and blend. Place on top of crumbs, and sprinkle with other half of crumbs. Chill before serving.

GAMES: Selecting Seeds

Divide into two teams. Provide teams two toothpicks for each player. Place a watermelon seed (or some large seed) in a cup for each player — each team has a cup with seeds in it. Using two toothpicks like chopsticks, players must pick up one seed from the cup, lay it on the table, and let the next player take his place. When all seeds are removed from the cup, the team finishing first wins.

Art Gallery Promenade

Give each player a sheet of paper with picture titles upon it. Each title is numbered, as are the various "art" displays around the room. They must match the numbered title with the displayed article.

1. The lonely beat	1. A single beet
2. The swimming match	2. A match in a dish of water
3. Peacemakers	3. Scissors
4. Grub that makes butterfly	4. Biscuit
5. Letter carrier	5. Envelope
6. The colonel's home	6. A corn cob
7. Four carat ring	7. Four carrot rings with center removed

SUPPLEMENTAL PROGRAM NO. 4
THEME — NEW LIFE

THOUGHT FOR THE MONTH:

"We were buried therefore with him by baptism into death, so that as Christ was raised from the dead by the glory of the Father, we too might walk in newness of life."   Romans 6:4

HYMN: "We Would Be Building" #489

SCRIPTURE READING: John 3:1-17

MEDITATIVE THOUGHT: New Life

Christian "new birth" is a phrase that has troubled and puzzled men for many generations, yet it draws the clearest picture of what Christianity should do in the life of a Christian, of any words that the Master might have used.

Jesus showed us a new way of life, a way so new and startling that it altered a world; a way so strange that men called him a radical, and the religious leaders of his day condemned him as a religious fanatic.

Our Lord exemplified in His earthly life the ideal of sacrificial living for others, and He asked us as Christians to follow Him into this new sacrificial way of life.

Birth is a forgetting of old ways, with the slate wiped clean of old offenses. The new birth means that we should start our Christian life with the purity, wonder, love and faith of the new-born baby. As the new babe is dependent upon his parents for his every need, so we should realize our complete dependence upon God. We should be ready to learn to accept His ways and His teaching and His leading, as the baby is ready to learn to accept the ways of this world as taught by his parents.

As the baby takes his first, faltering steps, clinging tightly to his parents' hands, may we cling close to our God as we take faltering steps in the new way we have chosen to follow. As we stumble, and sometimes fail in our high resolve, may we always know that our Father, God, stands ready to lift us to our feet again and encourage us to try again.

So let us follow the new way, the sacrificial way that Jesus led, learning to serve our fellow man, and thus fulfilling the law of Christ that we, too, might walk in newness of life.

PRAYER:

Our Father, wilt Thou help us to walk in that newness of life which distinguishes the true Christian from the ways of the world. Help us to be worthy of that name "Christian", and teach us to follow our Master with the trust and love of newborn babes. These blessings we would ask in His name. Amen.

HYMN: "Spirit Of God, Descend Upon My Heart"   #272

BENEDICTION:

Now, to Him who is the way, the truth, and the life, be everlasting glory, and honor, and blessing, from all creation as His followers strive to be worthy to name Him Lord. Amen.

SUGGESTIONS FOR THE HOSTESS

DECORATIONS:

Purple and white tulips in a low bowl, or a potted tulip plant may be used. Purple or white candles in tall candle holders.

REFRESHMENTS:

Black raspberry or black cherry Jello, cut into cubes and piled in sherbet glasses. Moisten a package of cream cheese with milk or cream, and add vanilla and sugar to taste. Place a teaspoon of the cheese mixture on top of each dish of Jello, and serve with a slice of plain loaf cake and coffee. A bowl of bright colored hard candies adds a touch of color and taste.

GAMES: Who Was He?

Clues: Deduct 10 points from perfect 100% score for each clue that has to be given before the name is guessed.

1. He lived in the land of Uz
2. He was a "perfect and upright man"
3. He was very wealthy; and he had seven sons and 3 daughters
4. His sons and daughters were slain, and he lost his wealth.
5. He was greatly afflicted with boils.
6. Three special friends came to comfort him.
7. He put on sackcloth and ashes in his grief.
8. God again gave him wealth — twice as much as before.
9. God again blessed him with 7 sons and 3 daughters.
10. He lived 140 years after he regained his prosperity.

WHO WAS HE? ———— Answer JOB

Christ Is Risen

Give out pencils and paper to all persons present. Let them write the words "CHRIST IS RISEN" across the top of the paper. See who can spell out the greatest number of words, using only the letters in the three words given at the top of the page. No proper names should be allowed.

SUPPLEMENTAL PROGRAM NO. 5

THEME — IN THE BEGINNING

THOUGHT FOR THE MONTH:

"In the beginning God created the heavens and the earth. The earth was without form and void, and darkness was upon the face of the deep; and the spirit of God was moving over the face of the waters."

Genesis 1: 1-2

HYMN: "O God, Our Help In Ages Past"   #585
SCRIPTURE READING: Deuteronomy 6:4-18
MEDITATIVE THOUGHT: In The Beginning, God

In the beginning, God. What a tremendous, powerful, remarkable way for a book to begin! God is put first in our Bible. How it would change things in our world if God were put first in our lives!

Jesus said, "Seek ye first His kingdom and His righteousness, and all these things shall be yours as well." He was telling us, in the language of the day, that if we truly put God first, and make Him of primary importance, all lesser things will fit into their proper places in our lives.

Are we willing to take God with us into our work, our play, and into our budgets? Would we be proud to have Him see how we allot our time for religion, for meditation, and for prayer? Would we be glad to have Him sit in with us as we plan our finances and budget our giving?

If God were to ask us whether we were using the talents that He gave us for the glory of God, could we say that we were using them to the very best of our ability? Let us remember that the twelfth chapter of Romans lists many kinds of talents. "Prophecy, service, teaching, exhortation, contributing and mercy" are all considered talents. Even in our giving, we are exhibiting talent in the liberal and cheerful way in which we live.

Let us truly put God first. With the Bible, let us say, always, "In the beginning, God — "

PRAYER:

Our Father, teach us to number our days that we may always put Thee and Thy Kingdom first, that other things may take their rightful place in our lives. May we always be conscious that Thou must come first in our lives, before comfort, before luxury — before all the things of this world. Help us to follow Him who taught us that we must "seek first the Kingdom of God, and His righteousness", for in His name we pray. Amen.

SUGGESTIONS FOR THE HOSTESS

DECORATIONS:

Place a bowl of pink and brown zinnias in the center of the table, and use pink candles at either end. Brown pine cones (picked up from underneath the trees) would be effective around the flower bowl.

REFRESHMENTS:

Serve squares of ginger-bread with whipped cream, which has been tinted pink with vegetable coloring, and garnished with maraschino cherries. Accompany this with coffee, fruit punch, or iced tea, and pink and white candies in small bowls.

GAMES: Speeds They Can Go

Match the numbers with what you think is the proper answer.

1. Swallow	4. 49 miles an hour
2. Rabbit	7. 25 miles an hour
3. Cheetah	5. One mile an hour
4. White tailed deer	2. 45 miles an hour
5. Turtle	6. 60 miles an hour
6. Gazelle	1. 110 miles an hour
7. Man	3. 70 miles an hour

Bible Occupations

Find the name of the man or woman who worked in each of the following occupations.

	Answer:
1. A silversmith	Demetrius (Acts 19:24)
2. An orator	Tertullus (Acts 24:1)
3. A tentmaker	Paul (Acts 18:1-3)
4. A seller of purple	Lydia (Acts 16:14)
5. A tanner	Simon (Acts 10:6)
6. A publican	Zacchaeus (Luke 19:2)
7. A centurion	Cornelius (Acts 10:1)
8. A sorcerer	Simon (Acts 8:9)